# Introducing you to ...

# Jesus my Friend

## Eira Reeves

GW00514790

Hello, my name is Lily and this is Andy. We have many friends and we all play together.

Each day we try to help one another.
Sometimes it's quite hard!

Come and meet my family ...

Mummy, Daddy, my brother Max and my sister Chloe, Grandma and Grandad.

We all have a very special Friend.
His name is Jesus.

May I tell you about Jesus and why He is so special?

It all started a very long, long time ago when God made the world.

It was a beautiful place!

But some people spoilt it. They fought one another and were unkind.

God was very sad. So He sent His Son, Jesus, to the world. Jesus was born in a stable one very dark night.

Jesus grew up in Nazareth with His family: Mary, Joseph and His brothers and sisters. He began to show people how to live and to be kind to one another.

Jesus loved little children and He wanted them to know that God was their heavenly Father.

He healed many people ... those who were sick, or those who couldn't walk, see or hear.

Isn't that wonderful!

A day came when Jesus took all the wrong things we have done on Himself. He died on a cross so that we could be forgiven.

However, after Jesus died He came back to life again – His friends saw Him and spoke to Him! Isn't that great news!

Then He went back to be with His Father in heaven.

Jesus is alive today! He is with us, by the Holy Spirit, wherever we are and whatever we are doing.

Jesus could be your special Friend today –
would you like to know Him?
Let me show you how ...

It's easy to talk to Jesus – talking to Him is called praying.

Sometimes we do things that God is not pleased with (like lying, or being rude or unkind), and so we need to say sorry.

Ask Jesus to be your special Friend and tell Him that you love Him. Begin to trust Him in all you do. He will never let you down.

You can talk to Jesus every day, in the morning, afternoon or evening. He will always be with you.

Talk to Him when you are sad. Talk to Him when you are happy. Jesus will always listen.

It's good to look at the Bible which is full of stories about Jesus and other people who loved God.

Ask someone to read it to you.

Maybe go to a church and enjoy being with others who have Jesus as a Friend. You will learn more about Him too!

Isn't it great to know you have a new Friend called Jesus who will never leave you and will always love you?

Come and join our friends and family throughout the world. Jesus is a very special Friend to us all. Isn't that wonderful!

## A prayer to say:

*Dear Jesus,*
*I have heard about You and I would like to become Your friend. I'm sorry for the times when I've done things that have made You sad and unhappy, but if I ask I know You will forgive me.*
*Help me to always love You and trust You. Thank You so much that You will never leave me because You love me so much. Thank You that You want me to be Your friend too.*
*May I get to know You better every day.*
*Amen.*